From INVISIBLE to Visible

From INVISIBLE to Visible

Master the Art of Being Seen

RHONDA KAALUND

NEW YORK

LONDON • NASHVILLE • MELBOURNE • VANCOUVER

From INVISIBLE to Visible

Master the Art of Being Seen

Published in New York, New York, by Morgan James Publishing in partnership with Difference Press. Morgan James is a trademark of Morgan James, LLC. www.MorganJamesPublishing.com

ISBN 978-1-64279-339-0 paperback
ISBN 978-1-64279-340-6 eBook
Library of Congress Control Number: 2018913138

Cover Design by:
Rachel Lopez
www.r2cdesign.com

Interior Design by:
Bonnie Bushman
The Whole Caboodle Graphic Design

In an effort to support local communities, raise awareness and funds, Morgan James Publishing donates a percentage of all book sales for the life of each book to Habitat for Humanity Peninsula and Greater Williamsburg.

Get involved today! Visit
www.MorganJamesBuilds.com

Dedication

To the woman I'd walk to the end of the earth for,
my mother, Sandra Peterson.
I dedicate this book to you for *always* believing in me and
believing that I have exactly what it takes to impact the world,
on an intimate level, one person at a time.
Thank you for showing me how to believe
in myself and to believe in others.

Table of Contents

Chapter 1

Feeling Invisible

"If you are waking up with the sensation that there has got to be more in life … There is."
– **Steve Harvey**

If you're reading this book, perhaps it's because you're feeling invisible and are struggling to be seen. Or maybe you picked up this book because you know someone who is struggling to be seen. Feeling invisible can be very debilitating. It's like existing in a world and no one even notices you're there. People can't see your pain. And though pretending can be sustained for a little while, the pain associated with feeling invisible can get the best of you if it goes unaddressed. Feeling invisible affects every aspect of your life.

While many women are able to balance a healthy work and home life, this isn't the case for everyone. Take my former client, Anna, for example. Anna was feeling invisible both at work and at home. At work, she used to be on top of her game. She was the one everybody came to for advice. She was the one chosen for most of the special projects and assignments. She was the one getting all of the accolades. But something was going on with Anna that no one could put a finger on. She started withdrawing and was rarely involved anymore.

At home, Anna described her romance as less than perfect. She'd put on a few pounds and had hardly enough time to attend to her family's needs. She'd stopped going out on dates with her mate and had every excuse in the book not to engage in physical contact. However, she couldn't seem to put her mind to what was really going on. All she knew was that her idea of having a good time at home was to kickback and watch a few episodes of *Family Feud*.

Anna had low motivation to embrace change in a positive way. There was a time where in her career, she was project lead on everything. She was advancing in the company, had won Employee of the Year several years in a row, and was featured on the company's website for outstanding service more times than she could count. The energy she spent in the office perfecting her work came with the cost of ten-hour workdays with an additional five hours on the weekends; however, it seemed all worth it because Anna felt fulfilled. She was able to manage her home life despite her robust work schedule.

At home, Anna's romance had been top notch. She and her husband often had spontaneous romantic date nights. They'd go out on the town. They'd cook together and also take mini family vacations. It seemed she had plenty of time to spend with the family engaging in game nights, one of their favorite activities.

Then suddenly, all seemed to have gone awry. When Anna looked around, her closest colleagues had either obtained promotions or transferred in their careers. Anna was still putting in those 50- to 60-hour workweeks and had no satisfaction, nor had she felt appreciated for anything she had contributed. It seemed many of the new hires had more energy and were much younger. Anna felt she couldn't compete. She was no longer selected for special assignments. Anna felt overlooked. She felt invisible.

At home, the date nights began to turn into a chore. Anna would cancel going out at the last minute, making up an excuse about "feeling tired." When the plan was to do something at the house, Anna found other things that were "more important" like doing the laundry. Anna's daughter had submitted her commitment statement to the university of her choice so actually, having more time to enhance her marriage should've been on the horizon. However, at home Anna felt invisible too.

The price to pay for staying in a job where one feels invisible seems quite high. Anna knew that without job satisfaction, it would be impossible for her to be content. She knew that going to a job on a daily basis where she felt invisible could potentially spill over into her personal life, which it had. She knew that something would have to change in order to get there but just didn't know the "what" or "how."

Anna had been married for 18 years and Roger was the love of her life. He did everything for the family, making sacrifices and even being patient when Anna's behavior didn't warrant such. Anna wanted the romance back. She wanted to WOW him at home and bring back the reason why they fell in love in the first place. She'd often tell people the story of how they met and longed for that feeling again. Life for them on the outside appeared amazing but, on the inside, they were beginning to crumble.

Because of her determining nature, Anna was convinced that she could get her life back if she only knew what to do. If she once "amazed" them at work and "wowed" him at home, she could do it again. Anna loved the feeling of being the go-to person in the office. It was the euphoric feeling that spilled over to her once-amazing home life. Roger would see the enthusiasm and confidence Anna displayed, and use it as motivation for himself. Roger pulled a lot of his energy from her because her energy was so strong. There were times when he would help her with work, giving constructive feedback as she prepared her projects. She too would help him by providing feedback for the work he did on his job. They were a team, a strong team. Their romance never suffered because they were enjoying life. They looked forward to those encounters. They delighted in each other's company.

Anna wants to feel rejuvenated. She wants to be able to go into a job where she feels heard and valued. A place where she is contributing. She is not sure if her current career path is where she is supposed to be but what she does know is that she had what it took before and wants a transformation. She is tired of feeling invisible.

Chapter 2

I Know What It's Like

"It's hard being visible so I've made myself invisible."
– Danielle Steel

I never thought in a million years I'd feel invisible or even be in a position to fight to feel seen again. I didn't think I could find the proper word to fit how I felt, but once I connected to feeling *invisible*, I knew I needed a way to reverse that thought. My invisibility was different from Anna's. My invisibility was as a result of how I perceived my ability to write and speak. It was my lack of confidence.

Written and circled in bold red ink, the letters *A W K* for awkward must have appeared on almost every page of my ten-page term paper. I was a sophomore in college at Appalachian State University and had never received negative feedback from any written work submitted prior to then. I didn't consider myself a master or superior writer, but my English and Literature grades were great. Nonetheless, this would be a defining moment for me. I became extremely insecure about my writing and speaking skills. You see, this event, the red AWK written all over my paper, caused me to question my capabilities. I thought to myself that if my writing was awkward, my speaking had to be awkward too. Coming up with this conclusion kept me from showing up. I was hiding. On the one hand, I didn't want to be seen, while on the other, I was dying to be seen. So, I finished my academic careers, both undergraduate and graduate, with constant questioning and doing things over and over. I even limited my opportunities to speak.

Corporate America was no different. I had this inner struggle to be seen. Because I had conditioned myself to believe that what I had to contribute was unworthy and couldn't possibly add value to any situation, I often sat back and observed. There were times when I'd make a deal with myself and say, "Today you'll speak in this staff meeting, and your reward will be a Fossil bag." But it never worked. It was like my lips were moving but nothing came out. I was paralyzed. I didn't want to be judged. I was in total fear of receiving any form of feedback. I expected it to be negative. This fear was so great that I even left staff meetings to go to the bathroom when I sensed my supervisor was going to go around the table to get input from the group. And during the times I remained in meetings, I'd carefully customize a safe response like, "I agree with Toni, I do believe the students need an advocate with them to start the march." This seemed to minimize any possibility of negative scrutiny. I was so good at making myself invisible that I ultimately mastered denying my own voice. I was just too afraid and insecure to release it. What I regret the most are the times I was confident about adding value to discussions and missed them simply because I was afraid.

And you can imagine, writing was no different. I was skilled at hiding, so my most popular statement, "You're a fast typer, won't you please draft this for me?" could have won the award for the most used phrases in any one job setting. True, I was no fast typer, but it was an easy crutch. It allowed me to safeguard my insecurities. It was me who had interpreted my writing skills weren't good enough, so I hid. I chose to be invisible.

Being invisible was my little secret. At the time, it felt much better to feel invisible than to receive all those red AWK's. However, the price to pay for me feeling invisible came with internal consequences. I didn't feel genuine. If I wasn't feeling genuine, then I wasn't being true to myself. So, I needed to do something. I had a lot of proof that what I had to say added value. For example, just before my niece Cassie started college, I gave her the good ole auntie talk. Don't date—wait until you're married. Don't drink—unless you're having just one glass of wine, and don't party (well, not too hard), but study all the time. A few years after she graduated, she shared with me that she'd listened to everything I had to say and that she valued my opinion. But you can't just count family feedback. A former client called to tell me how much her life had changed from our work together. She now makes herself a priority and engages in self-care that has ultimately led to her increased self-confidence. Additionally, I've facilitated many trainings and workshops, have had weekly commercials on the local radio station, and have emceed many events, all without any thoughts of whether or not I could do it. In fact, I was receiving consistent positive feedback.

As a former Academic Advisor, I must have written at least thirty letters of recommendation, and I have also written several letters of reference for colleagues. At these requests, I never thought twice about what I was saying and never questioned its value. Students got into their graduate school programs and colleagues got their promotions. It was evident that my input did not stop them. As a licensed mental health and substance abuse counselor, I've written-up tons of psychosocial assessments and discharge summaries without reservation or hesitation. My clinical work during supervision had to be reviewed by a clinical supervisor and I've never received any critical feedback on my written performance. I've even taken a couple of postgraduate school courses and never had a problem. The proof was clear. I wasn't a crappy speaker, nor was I a crappy writer at all.

Chapter 3

The REDLIPSTICK Method

"The starting point of all achievement is desire."
– Napoleon Hill

One Sunday afternoon heading home from the grocery store, my husband Khari and I engaged in a conversation about red lipstick. I'd been on my cell phone scrolling through my Facebook feed when I noticed that several women were wearing red lipstick that day. It wasn't Mother's Day or some National Wear-Red-Lipstick Day, it just seemed to be a regular ole Sunday. None of these women were related or connected to my knowledge, so it was just plain interesting. They each owned their red lipstick in such a magical way that it was hard not to notice the confidence they displayed. I made the comment to Khari that the women wearing red lipstick were beautiful but that red lipstick just wasn't for me. He looked at me like I was a lil coo coo and began to challenge my assessment. Seems like he gave me a hundred and five reasons why it would look nice on me, and I gave him double the reasons why I disagreed. The conversation went on for several minutes and I was starting to get really defensive. Then I thought, maybe I should prove him wrong. So we decided to head to the mall, and I made a mad dash to the make-up counter. I looked through the various shades of red lipstick and purposefully picked out the one in which I thought would look the most hideous. After all, I had to prove my point that red lipstick did not compliment me. The sales associate began to assist me with the application of the lipstick and midway through the application process, I looked at Khari and he smiled. I thought to myself, he's either smiling because now he sees my point, or he's going to be nice and say it looks fine. Well, before I could utter another word, the sales associate shouts, "That looks amazing!" Not confident she was being truthful, I turned around in my chair, expecting to not be pleased.

I couldn't believe my eyes. I don't think I've ever been so surprisingly emotional at such a thing before. I agreed that the red lipstick looked amazing but my emotions had nothing to do with what I was seeing in the mirror. It had every bit to do with my rejection of myself. I had been working so hard to not put myself down. And in that moment, I wondered how many times in life I had rejected something that was truly meant for me. How many times had I said no to or dismissed something that I had never even given myself a chance to try? Could this have anything to do with my feeling invisible? Denying myself the chance to experience something new, to change or to grow, was a hard pill to swallow. Applying this red lipstick was so powerful and inspirational. And when I saw myself in the mirror, I had transformed. I didn't see wearing red lipstick as a way of literally being seen, but rather it was symbolic in how I transformed into a person who was ready to feel seen. Thus, this event would be the catalyst to the development of one of my coaching programs.

You see, I started thinking about when I felt invisible, when my confidence was low. It was my thought process that needed to change. It was my interpretation of how I was being perceived that kept me invisible. So, for the next few months, I had a deep desire to maintain this transformation. I painted often, I journaled a lot, I meditated, and I saturated myself with listening to my books on Audible. I listened all the time. I listened when I walked, when I traveled, and when I slept. Some of my books I listened to at least ten times. I learned something new every day. I started to implement what I was learning. Then it dawned on me that I had all of the skills required for transformation, but I just needed a process to follow. Because of my newfound awareness with my red lipstick moment, I developed that process. This process would be for you and for me. Many of my clients had gone through many of the steps with great results in the past, so I organized them and finalized the process. It is called The REDLIPSTICK Method.

The REDLIPSTICK Method is ideal for people who feel invisible or who have ever felt invisible and just want to feel seen again. Sometimes our invisibility shows up as the lack of confidence, guilt, unworthiness, addiction, weight problems, medical conditions, marital problems, depression, anxiety, fear, etc. No matter what your invisibility is or is tied to, the following concepts in The REDLIPSTICK Method will give you guidance to help you master the art of being seen.

R **Release the stronghold**. A stronghold is any negative or faulty thinking that we've assumed to be true based on external stimuli. Strongholds do not serve our greater good, they only serve to keep us from moving forward into our destiny or purpose. This step focuses on identifying and releasing those strongholds.

E **Embrace your authentic self.** Authentic self refers to who you are at the core. As William Shakespeare so eloquently wrote in his play *Hamlet*, "To thine own self be true." This step in the process allows you to figure out who you are so that you have a better understanding of how you can serve yourself and others.

D **Declare your purpose.** Your purpose is directly connected to knowing why you are here on Earth. Knowing why you were created is essential to living a full life. This step allows you to spend some time thinking about your purpose and taking ownership of it.

L **Lean into the process**. When you lean into the process, you follow a specific outline to help you establish goals that are connected to your life's purpose.

I **Imagine a new life.** If you imagine it, it can come to pass. In this step, the focus is the power of visualization to manifest that which you desire.

P **Practice affirming it.** Affirming something sets your subconscious mind to believe that whatever you are affirming is already in your possession. It takes practice, but when you speak it with confidence and you connect your emotions with receiving it, you'll be amazed at what you manifest.

S **Show up.** To show up is to be fully committed to that which you seek to change. It includes being physically present as well as being mentally present and is often accompanied by sacrifices.

T **Transform to the new you.** You will be transformed into the person you desire to be. You will learn how to own this transformation that has been grounded in your purpose.

I **Influence your surroundings.** Influencing your surroundings is often done subconsciously. In this step, you will see how you have affected and impacted those around you.

C **Celebrate accomplishments**. You will learn that celebrating your wins, your milestones, and your accomplishments is key to additional successes. It is all too often that we do the work but there is no celebration for the efforts we have put forth.

K **Kickback.** During the kickback phase, you will discover that by following The REDLIPSTICK Method, you truly can bask in the knowledge that you are no longer invisible and have mastered the art of being seen.

At the end of each section in The REDLIPSTICK Method, there are two different options for activities that are tied to each step. One is a general activity and the other is an optional Expressive Arts activity. Expressive Arts activities in this book include drawing, painting, collaging, face masking, vision boarding, journaling, poetry, dancing, and music to help cultivate deeper meaning for personal growth and development.

Although you are not required to complete the activities, many clients reported greater results when they engaged in at least one of the options.

Therefore, the prerequisite for moving forward is desire. So, as long as you have a strong desire to move from invisible to visible, you will master the art of being seen again.

Chapter 4

Release the Stronghold

"A belief is only a thought you keep thinking."
– **Abraham-Hicks**

My first understanding of a stronghold was introduced to me during a Sunday morning church service. Our minister referred to a stronghold as faulty thinking, something that we have developed in our minds that is not based on truth. In fact, he indicated that the adversary tricks us into believing that which is not true. We can either believe the faulty messages or reject them.

In 2015, I decided I was going to write a book. Not just any book, but one that would serve to help people reach their highest potential. I was passionate about working with people—encouraging, motivating, and mentoring them, so to get it out in book form seemed to be the answer. I was living in Europe at the time and was very busy at work. Most days I didn't get home until the evening and worked some Saturdays. But when I had a free moment, I had a date with the library. I was on a mission. I'd plug in my earbuds, listen to the newest book I had on Audible, and walk to the library. The library was the place where I spent most of my free time, so you could find me on the second floor, just past the newspaper section. I can still hear the accent of the German librarian as she'd smile at me and say "Guten Morgen" when I arrived on a Saturday morning or 'Guten Abend" on the rare occasion I was there on a weekday.

I probably have about three or four journals I've started writing but never had the time to finish. My number one cheerleader back then was Sherie Aaron, a lady I had met at a conference in Boston, MA. I shared with Sherie that I was writing a book and she volunteered to be my accountability partner. She'd check in with me to see if I'd made it to the library and, if I had, she'd check to see if I'd done any writing. I loved Sherie checking in on me because it was encouraging and it decreased the chances of me putting my writing off. Then life happened, and I moved back to the United States. It would be a whole year later that this message I wanted to get out to you would begin its conception again.

I had developed a method that would provide women all over the world the opportunity to make changes in their lives and have a tool to use to reflect back on it anytime they needed it. My goal was to have the book out by the end of 2018. If that was going to happen, I was going to need a coach. Investing in myself hadn't always been a priority, but over recent years I had grown to see the tremendous benefits. The more I invested in myself, the better I would be at serving from a higher place of excellence. To make sure I would produce the best product I was capable of producing, I searched for a coach. Not just any coach—I wanted the best one in the industry. I did my research and began working with Dr. Angela Lauria with the Author Incubator. My book would be ready in a few short months.

When it was time to write, I picked up my pen, then I put it down. I wasn't ready. I pulled out my laptop and began to type, but nothing came out. I grabbed my recorder and began to dictate, only to find that I would erase it. What was the problem? Why was I having so much trouble? Then I started to ask questions like, "Who are you to write this book? What qualifies you to be the expert?" I was shocked because I could not understand what was blocking me from getting this done. Then, boom—guess who showed his ugly face? The big red AWK. Visions of AWK kept popping in my mind. What is this? I couldn't believe it. I thought I'd moved past feeling invisible and inadequate and insecure, etc. But it showed up again. After spending some time thinking about this, I realized that AWK was the stronghold that was keeping me from moving forward. I knew I needed to release it. I revisited the validity of the meaning I gave to AWK. I had too many instances to rely on that proved AWK to be faulty thinking. And because the first step in The REDLIPSTICK Method starts with our thought process, I was able to identify those negative thoughts and release them because they did not belong to me. You see, it's not uncommon to think you're not good enough at something in life, but the power is in whether or not you believe that thought to be true. I am a contributing author in the book *The Love Pact*, so questioning whether or not I could write this book was absurd. Once I released those thoughts and rejected ownership of them, this project took off. If I was able to release my stronghold to get this book done, I'm confident you will be able to identify your stronghold and ignite the fire you need to move you into your destiny, just like my client Mechelle.

Mechelle had taken a job overseas. She had planned to move with her husband and three children; however, her oldest son, age 18, chose not to move. Mechelle wanted to empower him to make his own decisions but it was killing her to leave him behind. She was plagued by guilt. Her guilt was so heavy that she purposefully avoided indulging in travel and experiencing the European culture because she thought doing so would be perceived as fun and she didn't want her son who stayed behind to feel left out. Mechelle thought that if she engaged in anything fun, it would be a betrayal to him; thus, she began to isolate herself. When she and I worked together, Mechelle was able to identify guilt as her stronghold. She was able to process the validity of her thoughts and was able to release it. Mechelle was able to see that it was her mindset that was holding her back and opportunities for global understanding and personal growth had been hindered. Once Mechelle worked through the stronghold and had a better understanding of how to recognize and release it, her progress catapulted to new heights.

Another one of my clients, Dee, experienced years of incessant disappointment and lost the ability to forgive. She made conscious decisions to never pardon anyone, even when the offense had been unintentional. Eventually, the desire to never forgive even the tiniest of conflict began to imprison her relationships. She had gone through life viewing her inability to forgive as strength rather than a stronghold. When introduced to The REDLIPSTICK Method, she learned to release the negative thinking and made allowances for those who'd hurt her. She used her writing skills to journal through this process.

How to Release the Stronghold

Over the years and specifically because of the work that I do with people, I've mastered eliminating faulty thinking and have helped so many others do the same. Anna, my former client introduced in Chapter 1, felt invisible at home and at work. Her feeling invisible had every bit to do with how she was interpreting what was going on from within. At work, Anna was feeling left behind and uncertain that she was capable of pursuing anything greater or even improving her skill set on the job. It was easier to claim that she was being overlooked or that others were getting the attention. What she discovered was that she had fear. Fear was stopping her from moving into her greatness. With her daughter heading off to college, Anna reported feeling "old" and, because she had picked up a few pounds, she concluded that her husband was less attracted to her. Nothing about her skill set changed, it was her own interpretation of it. Nothing changed at home. Her husband loved her more and more each day. It was her faulty thinking that got her to believe that she was no longer being seen. When Anna realized that it was her own thought process that got her to that point, she was ready to do some work. Anna delighted in identifying what she felt she needed to change in order to release the faulty thinking she had developed. I worked with her through coaching sessions. She identified what she believed to be true that was consistent with her feeling invisible. They were her own insecurities. She recognized that once she was able to identify what those thoughts were, she felt more secure. Engaging in activities to identify and release the strongholds is cathartic. She discovered that not only was happiness a choice, but also being at peace and being confident were choices she could make as well. These were key to her being seen again.

Activity: Release the Stronghold—Letter to Self

Purpose: Identify the strongholds that you feel are hindering you from moving forward. Writing it out in letter form helps connect you with releasing them.

Suggested Materials: Pen, paper, and an envelope OR journal and pen OR word document on computer or tablet

Directions: Find a quiet place and create a mood conducive to writing. Address the letter to yourself and write in third person, identifying the strongholds that are you are releasing. Then talk about what this process was like for you. Seal the letter, close the journal or store what you typed, and revisit it after twelve weeks or when you have completed The REDLIPSTICK Method twelve-week program.

Optional Expressive Arts Activity: Release the Stronghold—Tree Story

Purpose: Identify the strongholds that you feel you need to release and find things to replace them with. This sets you up for success and builds your confidence. Think of the things that are positive that complement the strengths you know you possess.

Suggested Materials: Multi-color pencils or markers, drawing paper (other options include paintbrushes, canvas and paint, or anything you choose to express yourself in this Release the Stronghold Tree Story.)

<u>Directions</u>: Draw a tree with limbs and branches. Draw leaves on the tree. Draw the base of the tree with many roots. Use the root extensions to identify your known strengths and the good qualities you possess. For the leaves, write the things in pencil that you are committing to leave behind, then put what you plan to replace that thing with in permanent marking. For example, if "complaining" is something you want to leave behind, then write out "complaining" in pencil and replace it with the word "gratitude."

In a Nutshell

You've always had the power to release a stronghold. You control what you think of yourself and how you interpret what others think of you. These beliefs belong to you. This journey is your journey and it's the beginning of the purification of your mind when you release those faulty messages. Take charge. If what you are thinking doesn't build, increase, or elevate you, then you have the power to change it. It's important that you think about what you want and who you want to be, rather than what you don't want or who you don't want to be. When we have visibility on how we perceive ourselves, we establish a great foundation for being seen.

Chapter 5

Embrace Your Authentic Self

"As you become more clear about who you really are, you'll be better able to decide what is best for you the first time around."
– Oprah Winfrey

"You are enough. You are more than enough." I see this message all the time posted on various social media outlets. What does it really mean? My initial interpretation was that perhaps this was a message of encouragement and motivation. Then I spent more time thinking about what it meant to me personally. No matter what I have experienced in life, there will always be moments and days where I'll be challenged. Some days I might challenge my abilities, while on other days I may feel unseen. It had been during those times that I put on a mask to present myself well to the world. In fact, when I wore that mask, I began to conform to what I didn't feel comfortable with. Conforming never felt authentic. Therefore, to attempt to alter the pure essence of who you are always comes with a price. Have you ever been in a situation where you were conforming?

During my mid-twenties, my sister Tabatha volunteered to coach me on how to break up with my boyfriend. He'd constantly tell me that I wasn't tough enough and needed to have thicker skin. My personality is pretty laid back so any signs of aggression were simply unusual for me. Because my sister was the assertive one, I took her up on the deal. The relationship was hitting several walls, so my sister thought I should ramp it up a notch and give him a piece of my mind. She wrote out quite the colorful script for me to say to make sure my point was made. I remember practicing the script over and over to give it the punch that it really needed. Once I mustered up enough confidence to deliver it, I gave him a call. He didn't even answer. His voice machine came on. Because I was so energized to deliver this message, I left the recording on the voice machine. It seemed like 60 seconds later my telephone rang, displaying his number. I nervously but with confidence picked it up, only to hear laughter in the background. The laughter was that of his mother and him. He was at her office at the time and apparently, he played the message on speakerphone so that she could hear it as well. His mother and I were really good friends and I was totally humiliated for her to hear me speak in such a fashion. She told me that it was funny because it was so out of character for me. She reminded me that I didn't need to change or conform for anyone, for any reason. She proceeded to tell me that people love me just the way that I am. As silly as that sounds today, the meaning behind that interaction would stick with me for life. There is no need for me to change who I am for the benefit or comfort of another.

This revelation of embarrassing myself didn't just happen in a matter of five minutes of thought processing. It happened over time. With all of the things that have helped bring me to be the person that I am today, I had to master self-love. I had to be okay with being laid back and non-aggressive, and all of the other qualities that have somehow made me not confident.

When I started writing this book, I realized this step would be one of my favorites. I happened to see a Facebook post with a picture of me, my sister, and my cousin Caprice. I looked to be three years old. I saw innocence. I saw that we were carefree. And I wondered if that girl would be proud to know me today. Then I ran across a picture of myself when I was about ten years old. This picture was taken at my family reunion on my dad's side. I was so thin and appeared very self-conscious and insecure. Then I looked at a picture from a photo-shoot I had taken back in 2017. I looked happy and confident. I made a copy of each picture and placed them on one picture frame. This picture frame would serve as my motivation for transformation and change. It would be symbolic of me embracing my authentic self, me being comfortable with who I was at all three of those stages. I sat this picture next to my computer and looked at it every time I wrote.

In order to determine who I was at the core, I needed to answer this question: "What qualities or characteristics do I possess that others see as well?" It was important for me to ensure that the information provided in this book came to you from a place of love and compassion. So, I tested this theory. In fact, as I was writing this chapter I stopped and made a list of five qualities about myself and sent the following message out to ten people who know me well, soliciting their responses. "If you had to use five words to describe me or my character, what would they be?"

I didn't realize how powerful this assignment was going to be for me because I had only given it to my coaching clients in the past. When we processed it, they'd tell me that the solicited responses were very similar to the list for qualities they had written out for themselves. This experience was invigorating for me. I expected the responses to be similar but I wasn't quite ready for how the responses would make me feel. Every person's response had at least three qualities that I had on my list. This assignment confirmed how I thought I was seen by others. I felt more confident and secure as a result of doing this simple task and it further motivated me to continue writing.

But what if some of the qualities you've listed for yourself are things that you aren't pleased about? For example, one of my clients said she felt invisible all of her life, in her family, and at work. Words she used to describe herself were worthless, failure, invisible, and loser. She assumed that what other people thought of her would be the same. When she did this exercise, people's responses were: helpful, compassionate, generous, determined, and caring. This gave a major boost to her self-esteem. It allowed her to question those negative qualities she outlined for herself and begin to embrace the good in how others saw her. She was able to see the truth in all of the descriptive words that were given to her. However, on the flip side, if most people are telling you things that are negative and new to you, you can spend some time processing them to figure out if there are in fact some things you need to change. If this occurs, connecting with a coach to help you through this is great.

When my client Dee worked through this step, embracing her authentic self meant reevaluating her core values. Her inability to forgive others revealed an inability to trust herself. She wanted to change, so spending time in this step opened her mind to explore a more compassionate approach to how she interfaces with others. Now, there are no suspicions of mistrust at the onset. She engages in relationships, getting to know people as people first without suspecting they have underlying intentions.

Society can inadvertently tell us what we should or shouldn't do, how we should or shouldn't behave, and we develop ourselves based on that knowledge. I have embraced my authentic self. I am at peace when I am myself. When I have tried to change who I was and conform to the person someone else expected or wanted me to be, it didn't feel natural. I was out of balance and out of sync. Our body has a way of telling us when we are. We'll experience physiological symptoms when we do. Looking back to that disastrous call to my boyfriend, I spent time practicing so that I could perfect that script. No matter how much I practiced to perfect it, the message came out untrue and unauthentic. I didn't feel like I was the person talking. My heart was pounding and my hands were sweating. All clues, right?

Can you think of a time in your life when you felt fake and unauthentic? What happened that alerted you that you were not your authentic self? If you were able to turn it around, how did you do so?

How do you embrace your authentic self?

Once you are able to identify your core qualities, move in that truth. Embracing your authentic self means accepting and loving "you" wholeheartedly. If you do the assignment and find that one quality stands out and isn't supported by your view or anyone else's, you can choose to reject it. Many times, people project their stuff onto you and it could very well be their own quality they need to work on. If a majority provide descriptions that are surprising to you, spend some time digging deeper to see if in fact it is something that holds some truth. If you want to change it, you have the power to do so. You are the author of who you are and who you desire to be, so embrace your authentic self and make changes when you discover that there is something within you that is no longer serving you.

Activity: Embrace Your Authentic Self—Character Traits List

Purpose: To determine who your authentic self is based on your beliefs and feedback from others.

Suggested Materials: Pen and paper

Directions: Spend some time thinking about the kind of person you believe yourself to be. Think about how you would describe yourself or how you believe others would describe you. If you believe what they have said to be true, use them to help build your list of five qualities. Then, solicit, from ten other people who know you well, their thoughts about you. Use the prompt, "If you had to use five words to describe me or my character, what would they be?" Compare the list they came up with and the list you created for yourself. Use this exercise to embrace your authentic self. Examine the consistencies. Accept that which serves you and be true to yourself on the qualities you find you need to change.

Optional Expressive Arts Activity: Collage

Purpose: To have a visual of something that helps you to see yourself. It serves as a reflection you can connect with.
Suggested Materials: Face mask, cardboard, stock paper or poster board any size. Magazines, images, or pictures depicting these qualities, scissors, and glue
Directions: Set a mood for creativity. Create a collage that represents who you are at the core. Choose and cut out images that match the qualities you've determined or discovered for yourself. Arrange images onto the paper and glue.

In a Nutshell

Only you have the power to truly identify who you are at the core. Use those words to embrace your authentic self. Own those words that serve "you." This is who you are at the core. When you are able to identify who you are and embrace your authentic self, you are more focused and can see more clearly and thus can make the best choices for your life. It is the starting point to erasing the feelings of invisibility.

Chapter 6

Declare Your Purpose

"Everything in the universe has a purpose. Indeed, the universe intelligence that flows through everything in a purposeful fashion is also flowing through you."
– Wayne Dyer

Have you ever worked a job where you pulled into the parking lot and sat there until the clock struck three minutes before the time you were scheduled to start? Have you rubbed your stomach from the buildup of knots only to find that for lunch you were going for the antacid? Have you dreaded Sunday nights and rejoiced Friday mornings? If you answered yes to these questions, I feel you. I was in that environment for forty hours a week. It wasn't that I couldn't do the job, but rather I wasn't the person purposed to execute the mission. Fortunately for me, it was only for a few months; however, many people experience this time and time again.

In 2001, I was working for the University of North Carolina at Chapel Hill. My friend Toni asked if I wanted to join her in reading *The Purpose Driven Life* by Pastor Rick Warren. I was excited about reading the book because at that time in my life, I wondered if I was moving in my purpose. I was heavy into church and didn't mind the long drives on Thursday nights for Bible study, Saturday mornings for dance practice, and Sunday afternoons for church service. In fact, spending time driving was a way for me to connect with the Divine. I considered the travel time a privilege and used it to pray.

When reading *The Purpose Driven Life*, I discovered that I was moving in the right direction. I was serving others in a way that brought me peace and I felt fulfilled. I felt like I was making a difference in the lives of those around me.

One of my favorite jobs was as the coordinator for a minority recruitment program for a pharmacy school. One of the missions of this position was to help the school diversify its student enrollment in the field of pharmacy. A perfect assignment for my colleague Randy and me! He was great with recruiting the students and I was an excellent relationship builder, so together the two of us created dynamic relationships with many universities across the US. We were very successful in our recruitment efforts to get students to apply to the university. We were instrumental in pioneering the pharmacy school's first summer camp program and our efforts contributed to increased enrollment for minority students. Things were going well until the period when the grant dollars dissolved. It was a pilot program so we understood that the funds ending were inevitable. What would this mean for me? I was offered a different position within the pharmacy school. I was coordinating the continuing education program for pharmacists across the state. I loved the people I worked with and the tasks at hand; however, the functions of the job were not challenging enough for me. I was accustomed to working with people in the capacity of counseling, teaching, recruiting, and academic advising. The many administrative duties for this position were important; however, executing them was not my passion. My purpose was serving people.

I knew I needed to make a decision about the job. My salary was higher than any other job I had held at the time, so considering leaving was indeed scary. As with any tough decision you have to make, you always think about the consequences and how it will affect and impact your family. After a long discussion with my family, I confidently gave my letter of resignation. Why confidently? I knew that my time had ended. I was no longer serving people. I was serving a system, but what I needed was to be in the presence of people. My purpose was to help people change, develop, and grow organically. I needed to be able to speak to the incredible uniqueness of individuals. To be a vessel to help them discover the greatness that resided within them. I discovered my purpose from being in tune to what other people said they appreciated about me. I found that strangers would come up to me and feel compelled to share some of the most personally tragic stories, and after a few moments of talking, they'd say how much better they felt. Creating that space for even strangers to feel unconditional love and acceptance is exactly where I thrived. I knew I was in my purpose helping people heal emotionally and assisting them in becoming the best version of themselves. Therefore, it was easy to leave the job at the pharmacy school to pursue full-time engagement in the behavioral health field.

Not soon after that experience at the pharmacy school, I developed my personal mission statement. During a Sunday church service, we had a guest speaker who challenged the congregation to develop their personal mission statements. It would be the first time I actually gave it deep thought and wrote it out: "I will extend myself and my circle of influence to help enhance the value in you." I loved it because it spoke to how I engage with family, friends, and clients. Over the years, I have revised it; however, it still holds true to this basic premise. Having my mission established made it easier to put my purpose statement into words. I had to go back to what I had read in the *Purpose Driven Life* to truly articulate what I believed to be why I was created. I was created to serve people. How could I capture it in a statement that is congruent with how I defined my authentic self? My purpose: I was created to help bring people to the realization and the manifestation of their truest highest potential. This statement is in a place I can see every day—in my office, in my den, and captured on my phone. Reading it ensures that I am not invisible. I am not invisible to the people that I serve and I am not invisible to me.

Like Dee, my client Kathryn felt that being invisible served a purpose for her as well and she prided herself in it. Kathryn felt attacked emotionally by many people who should have been important supporters in her life. Kathryn felt broken mentally, physically, emotionally, and spiritually. She felt fearful when standing in her own power and because of this, Kathryn's stealthy ways had become her literal survival tools to keep others from attacking her. However, through searching for her purpose, Kathryn was able to see that her life's mission shifted to knowing that there is more positivity in being seen than unseen. She embraced her authentic self and now refuses to tiptoe around anyone or anything that challenges the work she's done when she released her stronghold and embraced her authentic self. Kathryn is living more courageously and confidently. She realized that her life's purpose is founded on unconditional love. Because of that, Kathryn has forgiven and continues to love those who have hurt her. Although they are not in her life, she is able to move forward because of this unconditional love.

How do you declare your purpose?

Declaring your purpose is essential to being seen. To do so, you must seek within your heart to answer the question, why were you created? What is the purpose of your existence? Spending some time meditating on this can help you discover your purpose. Think about the things that you do that bring joy to others. Usually when we are serving others through our divine purpose, we get joy and feel at peace from helping them. When I decided to write this book, I knew that it was connected with my purpose. If I can transform to become a better me, I knew I could get this information to you in book form to help you become a better you.

Activity: Declare Your Purpose— Write Out Your Purpose Statement

Purpose: To have a visual of your life's purpose and to manifest a connection with you.
Suggested Materials: Writing utensil and paper or computer
Directions: Write out or type out your life's purpose. If you are not sure, use the following questions to help guide you in developing and declaring your purpose.

1. What do most people seek your help for?
2. What do you do in life that is fulfilling?
3. If you could do anything in the world and leave a legacy, what would it be and why?

Optional Expressive Arts Activity: Purpose Expressed

Purpose: Painting is very therapeutic. You are in the present moment and you connect with your emotions. It is a soothing exercise that allows you to connect with your creative self. Spend a few moments to reflect on your life's purpose, visualize, and paint an image depicting it.

Suggested Materials: Paint, brushes, canvas

Directions: Set the mood with relaxing music. Clear any distractions and paint.

In a Nutshell

In order to build a strong foundation for yourself, you must subscribe to something greater than you. This causes you to be a better person. It allows you to leave this world a better place. Align yourself with people who affirm the person you are or are becoming. This is essential for maximum impact. When you can define your purpose and own it, you will begin to feel more visible. Once you believe in yourself, you are unstoppable.

Chapter 7

Lean in to the Process

"Begin with the end in mind."
– Stephen Covey

Watching some of the 2018 Winter Olympics was a great treat. It was especially nice because my niece, Cassie, was in PyeongChang to see some of the events live. This meant I got a play-by-play commentary from a trusted family member. One of the events that I especially love to watch is the ski jump. Ski jumping is a competitive sport in which the jumper skis down a steep ramp in a crouched position, accumulating as much speed as possible, and when the skier reaches the takeoff point, he leaps outward and upward, covering as much horizontal distance in the air as possible as he strives to his destination. Picture that. That ski jumper is going somewhere.

He has a strategic set up for the best possible results. Now that you have released the stronghold, embraced your authentic self, and declared your purpose, it's time for you to lean into the process. Just like the ski jumper has a strategic set up for the best possible results, this step when followed will give you the best possible results for achieving goals.

At the start of each year, one of the things that I have been able to master is setting goals. I would set weight-loss goals and begin each January ecstatic about dropping some pounds. I would be the first person to sign up for one of those programs like Curves, Weight Watchers, or even purchase a few books on green smoothie diets. The first few months were always successful with a loss of 15-20 pounds, but then life would get in the way. Work travel would come up, birthday parties would happen, or visitors from out of town would arrive. When you live in Europe, visitors wanting to see Paris is a must. Have you ever tried to stick to a green smoothie diet while traveling in Paris?

The problem I had with unsustained weight loss was not having a systematic way of ensuring success. I failed to incorporate a checks-and-balances system that would take into account those types of distractions. Because of the lack of a systematic way to keep the weight off, I was constantly on the weight loss seesaw of up 10 pounds, down 5 pounds, up 10 pounds, down 2 pounds, up 10 pounds, down 1 pound.

It wasn't until I was able to develop a solid method that would allow me to connect my goals with my true purpose. I tested that theory in 2016. I wanted to enhance my professional skills in the area of training. I had already sought certification as a Laughter Yoga Leader and wanted to take that skill set to another level. I determined that obtaining the Laughter Yoga Teacher certification from the Master Guru himself, Dr. Madan Kataria, would be exactly what I needed; however, limiting thoughts came into play. You remember the strongholds I talked about that have a way of creeping up from time to time. Since I was pretty good now at releasing strongholds, I rejected those limiting thoughts and followed my method for setting and achieving goals.

Although goals and purposes are not synonymous, they do go hand in hand. Goals are more specific and they can work to serve your life's purpose. What I found to be true is that once I identified my life's purpose, my goals were much easier to establish. I was better able to achieve them and I could serve people on a higher level. So, let's talk about leaning into the process.

Developing a Theme (Word or Phrase)

Right before the start of a new year, many of my clients work on goal setting. I walk them through this process. I challenge my clients to think about a word or a phrase that resonates with them to use as their theme for the year. I ask them to spend a little bit of time thinking about this because this word or phrase will serve as their motivation. I have clients revisit their purpose statement and sometimes words or phrases from the purpose statement help them develop their theme for the year. Once that word or phrase is identified, clients are instructed to use it throughout the year as they note their successes. Pam, one of my coaching clients who was working on her marriage, chose the word FAITH. She was believing that she and her husband would be able to salvage their marriage. One of the things she did to seal the FAITH image in her mind was to purchase signs and blocks that spelled out FAITH and post them at work and at home. She held on to the belief that things could change, and they did. Their marriage improved tremendously over the year; in fact, they are now looking at renewing their vows. Other examples of theme words clients have used include Mechelle's ENGAGE, which is connected with her purpose of bringing positivity to the workplace and influencing others to reach their full potential. Another coaching client, Haven, chose the word READY. She was ready to address unresolved emotions and move forward in life. And my word was MANIFEST, and it was often accompanied by REDLISPTICK because I was determined to get this process out to you.

Adding a Mission Statement

Next, we work on developing a mission statement. In this process the purpose statement and mission statement have two very different meanings. Again, the purpose statement answers the question, "Why do you believe you were created?" and the mission statement answers the question, "How are you going to make the purpose happen?" For example, my 2018 theme of "Manifest" connects with my purpose of, "I was created to help bring people to the realization and manifestation of their truest, highest potential in every aspect." My mission statement is, "I will extend myself and impart my wisdom, influences, and resources to help increase the value in you." It's important to have your purpose, theme word, and mission statement within reach, because they help drive the goal-setting process.

Establishing Goals

Life and Business Strategist Tony Robbins, said that, "Setting goals is the first step in turning the invisible into the visible." I love that quote because moving from a place of feeling invisible to a place of being seen has purpose. Setting goals permits you to think about what it is you really want. When you write goals, you want to write them in a way that will help you have the greatest chance of achieving them. The following is a checklist on goal-setting.

1. Choose something that you are capable of achieving.
2. Be clear about what you want to achieve and write it in specific terms.
3. Make sure the goal connects with your purpose.
4. Establish a date to achieve your goal.

Identifying Relevant Objectives

In the Lean Into the Process step, we take it a bit further. Once clients have established their goal, I work with them to identify specific objectives that can keep them on track of meeting their goals. Objectives are the blueprint to achieving the goals. Since you have knowledge of my Theme, Purpose, and Mission Statement, let me share what a sample goal would look like.

Goal: "By August 30, 2018 I will have published *From Invisible to Visible. Master the Art of Being Seen.*" This goal was something I was definitely able to achieve and it was written in clear terms. It is connected to my purpose and it had a deadline. Goals and objectives are always adjustable; therefore, in this example, if I hadn't met that deadline indicated, I could have simply revised it. A sample objective for this goal would be: "Identify an editor and publisher for my book by May 8, 2018." Here again, specific, with a date to achieve it. When I work with clients we get really detailed about the objectives, establishing time lines for them to optimize the chances of meeting those objectives. This can include creating daily or weekly to-do logs.

Relevance to the Purpose

The step of examining the relevance of the goal back to the purpose has meaning. When we are crystal clear about our purpose and we can set goals that support that purpose, we navigate through life in a state of visibility. We are seen to ourselves and we matter to those we affect or impact. If, for example, our goal happens to be career/work related, how do we use our purpose and mission to establish a goal in that area? Mechelle was able to bring about change to the workforce through positive leadership.

Affirm with Gratitude that the Goal is Already Achieved

The final piece for the Lean Into the Process step is affirming that the goal set has already been achieved. Claiming that it is already done gives our inner being an indication that the goal is indeed welcome in that space. Clients are then asked as they look at their goal sheets daily to read it out loud. They are tasked with confidently affirming that the goal that is connected to their purpose has been achieved. And finally, they are encouraged to say it with gratitude. For example: "I am very happy and thankful that I authored *From Invisible to*

Visible: Master the Art of Being Seen and that readers now have information that will help them become rejuvenated."

There are mixed schools of thought on whether or not you should share your goals with others. Making a public declaration of goals has its pros and cons. I've found that when coaching clients as they set goals, having someone to help hold them accountable has increased their chances of goal completion. Identifying an accountability partner, especially when the goals have been similar, increased the changes of goal completion and in some cases motivated the client to strive for more. In my twelve-week coaching program, we specifically outline those goals together and we assess if having an accountability partner outside of the coaching program is right for them. Just like Sherie checked in with me on a regular basis, when I started writing a few years ago, I'm confident I wouldn't have written a thing on paper without her motivation. When I hired a coach to write this book, you betcha I was more motivated. Not only was I more motivated, I got results faster.

How do you lean into the process?

To lean into the process of establishing purposeful goals, spend some time thinking about one to three things that you desire to accomplish. Be intentionally specific. Reflect back on your life's purpose and how it might connect you to it. Then use the checklist to establish your goals.

Activity: Lean into the Process Worksheet

(Email me at visible@rhondakaalund.com with the subject line "Worksheet" for your free downloadable worksheet.)

Purpose: To have a place to write all facets of the Lean into the Process goal formation.

Optional Expressive Arts Activity: Goal Coin/Stones

Purpose: To have something tangible and symbolic that is moveable and can be kept with you at all times.

Suggested Materials: 1.5- to 2-inch wooden coins or flat stones, magazines, images depicting goals, scissors, glue, mod podge, paint brush, carrying sack

Directions: Set the atmosphere for creating. Cut out images small enough to fit on your coins or flat stones that represent the goals you have set. On one side, glue the goal images. On the other side, write out or type out a shortened version of the goal with the set achievement date.

In a Nutshell

If you can see the end results when you start, leaning into the process through goal setting can get you there. Having an idea as to where you're going is an essential step to being seen. For example, if I had never worked to un-silence my voice, both written and spoken from my own faulty misinterpretation from a remark on a term paper, I wouldn't be writing this book in this moment. I no longer wanted to feel invisible, it made me feel unauthentic. In Chapter 6, you identified your life's purpose. You discovered exactly why you're here. In this step, you focused on establishing goals that complement your life's purpose. Those goals are achievable goals, with specific objectives that connect back to your purpose. Then you developed a theme. The theme provided the space that supports your goal. The theme was used as motivation and as a reminder of the path that you're on. Each goal was followed up with an affirmation and a gratitude statement. When you're able to set goals that are related to your life's purpose, you begin to appear more visible to yourself and to others.

Chapter 8

Imagine New Life

"Your thoughts are incredibly powerful. Choose Wisely."
– Joe Dispenza

Nervous, I handed the scrap paper to the testing proctor and asked if I could go to the restroom before she handed me the results of my licensing exam. I remember looking in the mirror with sweaty palms thinking, what if I didn't pass. The faith and confidence my mother had in me was so high that the thought of not passing was devastating. Then I recalled the, "It's already done, Rhonda. You just have to go through the process," statements she had uttered to me many times in the past. At this moment, those words would reign supreme. I spent a few moments reflecting on that. Historically, many people didn't pass this exam the first time and I knew quite a few who didn't pass the second time. This was my first attempt, so the pressure was on. In graduate school, I developed a system that worked for me to successfully pass exams, so I decided to use that same system and solicit a group of individuals who were also preparing for the exam to form a study group with me. It was set up like a part-time job. We'd meet as a group every Monday—Thursday evening from 5-9 p.m. at the local public library and carve out individual study time on our own on the other three days. My commitment to passing this exam the first time was extremely high and I was ready to bring everyone I knew with me to achieve this goal together. I must have emailed ten people. Four people replied stating they wanted to join the study group; however, only one person took the bait, my friend Gilbert. We were a force to be reckoned with. We were each other's accountability partners. Days that I didn't want to go, I went for Gilbert, and vice versa. The library staff knew us well and were rooting for us. On the rare occasion that either of us would miss, the library staff took note of the missing person and continued to bid us well. At the end of the study sessions, Gilbert and I would always talk about how it would feel when we receive our score reports with "passed" stamped on it. We'd visualize the exam proctor handing it to us and the looks on our faces when we learn that we'd passed. Since we were testing different days, we'd image the phone calls telling the other the great news. We also imagined exactly how we'd celebrate with our families for bearing with us during those study periods when we were not with them.

Remembering this, my confidence grew and I walked back in to obtain the results. The lady had a neutral look on her face as she handed me the folded score report. Nervous and excited I opened it up to see that not only did I pass, but I passed with a score higher than I expected. This held true for Gilbert as well. His score was off the charts. We celebrated with our families, exactly how we had imaged it.

There were several things that I learned in that process. I had to clear the path to release the strongholds. My strongholds came up not only during the preparation phase of taking the exam, but also while taking the exam. I had to say to myself, "You've got this," and repeat what my mother always says to me, "It's already done, Rhonda. Just go through the process." Being able to embrace my authentic self in the process of preparing for the exam came in the shape of letting individuals join at the eleventh hour. We had one week left before the exam date and the initial plan was to use the final week for individual review. However, because there was a need for others, we continued the group. It is my passion to help people as much as I can, so it was a pleasure to allow them to join us. My obtaining licensure as a mental health counselor was completely aligned with my life's purpose. It has allowed me to lean into the process and do the work that I have been called to.

At this point, you now know how to release the strongholds. You have the knowledge of how to embrace your authentic self. You have the power to declare your purpose. You're aware of how to lean into the process of establishing specific goals that align with your life's purpose, so now it's time to really dig into the process of imagining new life. If you can imagine it, it can come to pass. Think about something good that you've achieved in the past. Was it a new job or promotion? Was it closing on your new home? Did you finally pay off that high interest credit card, or did you purchase your dream car? Did that perfect mate ask you out on a date? Either way, I'm willing to bet you spent a lot of time and energy focusing on receiving that particular thing. In fact, you were probably smiling and feeling good as you thought about that one thing. You may have prayed about it or asked someone else to pray for you, but either way, lots of time and energy were spent on obtaining that thing.

Now, think about something that's recently happened that wasn't so good. Reflect back on your thought process about it. Were you thinking the worst? Did you doubt that something you wanted would come to pass? Did you engage in negative self-talk? Were you experiencing the negative physical emotions attached to doubt and disappointments? The reality here is that whatever we focus on, we tend to bring into existence. Even through day dreaming, our images tend to manifest. We tend to connect to the emotions of what we think about, and before long it manifests. It doesn't matter if it's good or bad, it's the thought that we're connecting to that manifests. When we manifest what we don't want, I like to think of them of the image traps. For example, we know that we want to be healthy, but we think about being overweight, and being overweight comes to pass.

When I started working with my coach, she sent out a welcome package. In it were a workbook and many fun items, but the one item that made writing this book so real for me was the copy of her book, *The Difference.* I'd never picked up a book that evoked so much emotion before. The way this book felt in my hand brought pure joy. I held the book close to my chest and immediately began to visualize holding *From Invisible to Visible: Master the Art of Being Seen.* Then I visualized you feeling the same way I felt when you hold this book in your hands. Holding that book evoked emotions of hope, happiness, confidence, and love, and I was so eager to get this book to you.

How do you imagine new life?

When I read *The Secret* and *The Power* by Rhonda Byrne, I fully understood the concept of connecting visualization to feelings. When you imagine something and connect with how it feels when it comes to pass, you're in a better frame of mind to receive it. It's not that it was an easy task, but I practiced all the time, visualizing my goals achieved and connecting with how it would feel when they came to pass. This exercise kept me in a positive mental state and I remained hopeful. However, I also learned that when I thought of what I didn't want, that came to pass too. Like when I was writing this book, there were days when I felt stuck. All I could think about was being stuck, then thinking about the deadline, and then feeling stuck all over again. My emotions were negative and my thoughts matched.

Think about the goals established in the Lean Into the Process step. Visualize them coming to pass and connect with how it feels. Imagine getting that promotion. What does your new office look like? Who's the boss now—is it you? What about going out on that fancy date? What are you wearing, and where is your date taking you? Can you see it? Can you feel it? Are you smiling? Practice doing this often. Practice so much that it is routine. When I set the goal to go to India, I imagined not only what it would look like, but also how it smelled and how the weather felt. Use all of your senses when you imagine a new life.

A few of my clients worked on this step through the use of vision boards. Staci, one of my coaching clients, created her board to help manifest many things. Two of her big desires were to move out of the country and to obtain her degree in business administration. She and her husband moved out of the country shortly after she developed her vision board, and she recently graduated with her degree. Staci kept her board where she could see it daily. She stated she believed her desires were coming, and so she set goals to help her manifest her desires. Once Mechelle's purpose was established, she was driven to make a vision board with her theme—ENGAGE. She described never forgetting the moment when she made it. She used a bright yellow piece of construction paper with a US map filled with people, and in bright bold letters it read, "Make the workplace cool again." She placed the board in her office on the side of a bookcase that faced her desk. She looked at her vision board every day and was grateful that her life's purpose was being fulfilled. And finally, Blanche used her vision board creatively by putting prayers next to it. She was looking for ways to bring about extra income. She looked at her board daily and visualized increased income. Before long, Blanche manifested a part-time job.

My vision board for this book was in the shape of desiring to manifest my RED LIPSTICK project. I created two boards before finding a coach. At the time, I didn't have a title for my book, but I knew that whatever book it was going to be, it was going to connect with red lipstick. Not only did I do a vision board, I also often sat and relaxed with soft music, visualizing this process and this book coming to pass.

Activity: Visualization Exercise for Imagining New Life

Purpose: To connect images with senses.

Suggested Materials: Comfortable spot and favorite soft instrumental music

Directions: Sit in a relaxed position or lay down in a comfortable spot. Play soft instrumental music and imagine new life. Take regular breaths in and out, imaging how it will feel when this goal or dream manifests. Connect with all your senses as you imagine how it will look, sound, smell, feel, and/or taste.

Optional Expressive Arts Activity: Vision Board

Purpose: To have something reflecting your new life that you can visually see.

Suggested Materials: Poster Board 11x14, magazines, images depicting new life, scissors, and glue

Directions: Set the mood for creativity. Cut out images, words, phrases, etc. that represent your new life. Arrange on poster board and glue.

In a Nutshell

There is power in visualization. Your thoughts are the architects of your destination. How you feel is connected to your outcome. Think about what you want versus what you don't want. Think big, dream big, believe big, and do big. Choose wisely. This is an active ingredient to mastering the art of being seen.

Chapter 9

Practice Affirming It

"Everything that happens to you is a reflection of what you believe about yourself."
– Iyanla Vanzant

The day I discovered the power of affirmations, I was sold on making it a consistent practice.

I realized that through its use, I was the creator of manifesting the things I wanted. I am who I say I am, I have what I say I have, and I can do what I say I can do. This was discovered back in 2013.

I was offered a job that required me to move to Europe. One of the major responsibilities was to provide trainings to large groups of individuals, up to 100 people or more at times. Training was not an issue but the term "large group" stoked enormous fear in me. Just the thought of entering a room filled with that many people caused my hands to sweat profusely and my heart to pound rapidly. There were days where I wondered if I had accepted the wrong job. I even contemplated going back to the US because I was very nervous and very insecure about that portion of the job. I remember going to the hotel where Khari and I stayed when we first arrived. I was so anxious that I'd wait in the hallway until I got myself together. I was too afraid to share with him how insecure I felt because he wasn't completely sold on moving to Europe in the first place. I wondered if I'd even be able to muster up enough confidence to deliver those trainings. I insecurely shared my concerns about training large groups with one of my colleagues and, because she was so confident in me, she simply replied, "Oh, you've got this."

Why was I so fearful? I was physically not good enough. That was the mistruth I'd fed into my psyche many years ago. I carried the insecurities with me about body image all the way from my early childhood. I was teased for being too skinny and was referred to as "Skinny Rhonda." As a result, I developed an insecure complex about my body. To stand in the presence of a large group of people created anxiety. I felt the larger numbers increased the possibility of me being criticized about my weight. In high school, I weighed 103 pounds at five feet seven inches. And more than 20 years later, I'd gained over 100 pounds, so to think that someone would have issue with me being "skinny" was simply ludicrous.

Then, one morning, I was listening to a 30-minute podcast by Pastor Joel Osteen. The topic was about the power "I am." I loved what I was hearing, so I developed a routine of saying affirmations while driving to and from work. I thought about my insecurities around presenting in front of large crowds, so my affirmations went like this: "I am capable, I am comfortable, I am competent, and I am confident." Before long, it became automatic for me every time I got into the car. Then one day I noticed something had changed. I felt capable, comfortable, competent, and confident. Soon after that, the big day came. I was asked to provide a two-hour training with the command group. This group consisted of about 45 people. No one really knew that I was working on my confidence, nor did they know about my insecurities. This was the moment. This was the day that my self-esteem had been waiting for. This was test time. Would I pass? I'd been given about a week to prepare. I did some breathing techniques and decided to incorporate hands-on activities and an expressive art activity. That was pretty risky to ask a group of high-ranking military officials to engage in artsy activities, but I was most comfortable there and went for it anyway. The training was a success. In fact, the Garrison Commander came up to me afterwards, shook my hand, and indicated how much he loved the training and the use of the expressive activity. Another high-ranking official sent an email to my supervisor telling him how much he enjoyed the training and that it had been by far the best training he had ever attended. Was I capable? Oh yeah. Was I comfortable? Absolutely. Was I competent? You betcha. And was I confident? Like a pro. My affirmations worked. I have held on to the Cs and have named them my Cs of Affirmations that get me results every time.

When writing this book, there were days where I didn't feel capable, comfortable, competent, or confident. But because I've mastered affirming what I desire, going to my Cs of Affirmations was perfect. It was like I could feel the insecurities dissolving away. I kept the same routine on my drive to work. I had the desire to make sure this book was written. I'd say my affirmations, connect with how it would feel to experience what I was affirming, and believe that it was so. Then my writing catapulted to new heights. It became a smoother process.

My coaching clients Blanche and Mechelle used affirmations to manifest the things they wanted. Blanche used affirmation with her vision board. As she looked at her board daily, she'd affirm out loud what she wanted. This yielded good results for her. Mechelle used her affirmations in journal format. She wrote them out and practiced saying them daily. They've been instrumental in assisting Mechelle with creating the positive workplace she has desired.

How do you practice affirming it?

What is it that you desire? You've gone through half of the steps in The REDLIPSTICK Method. Because you've imagined new life, affirming that it's already done sets your brain up to better receive it. Cultivating a positive relationship with your thoughts and words improves desired outcomes. State boldly and confidently what you desire after the words "I am." When you do so, you put authority to it and it soon manifests. Just believe what you are saying. The following is a simple step-by-step process to remember when practicing affirmations:

1. Desire: Identify and be passionate about what you are seeking
2. Believe: Believe that it will come to pass
3. Visualize: Imagine what it will look like when it manifests
4. Feel: Connect with the emotions of how it will feel when it comes to pass
5. Release: Speak or write out what you want to manifest

Activity: Practice Affirming It—I Am Exercise

Purpose: To help condition the mind to receive that which you desire.

Suggested Materials: Paper and pen, or journal and pen

<u>Directions</u>: Journal out words or phrases that follow I AM, listing all of the things that are true and that you wish to be true.

Optional Expressive Arts Activity:
I AM Creative Expression

<u>Purpose</u>: To help condition the mind to receive that which you desire and to have a creative visual as a reminder.

<u>Suggested Materials</u>: Poster Board 11x14, magazines, words depicting who you are or hope to become, scissors, glue

<u>Directions</u>: Set the environment conducive to creating. Place the phrase "I AM" somewhere on the page so that it stands out. Cut out words or phrases that depict who you affirm to be. Arrange on poster board and glue.

In a Nutshell

Words manifest. What you think and say, and how you feel about yourself and your circumstances, reflects your life. Ensure that your feelings are not strongholds. If you find that they are, you'll need to release them, then change those strongholds to what you desire for yourself. You can practice affirming how you want your life to be and it will begin to come into fruition. You'll have the added bonus of improved confidence and will see that this simple task is instrumental on the path of being seen.

Chapter 10

Show Up

"You are one decision away
from a completely different life."
– Mel Robbins

"You've got this. It's already done. All you have to do is go through the process." These are the famous phrases spoken to me by my mother, anytime I've ever undertaken a large task in life. It's her way of encouraging me and instilling her belief in me. I hold on to these phrases as if my life depended upon them. Oftentimes, I'll place them on stickies, write them in journals, or type them out on the computer. These phrases serve as reminders to me that anything I set my mind to, I can and will do. And I want you to own these phrases too.

The task of writing this book has had its challenges. But it has also been one of the most exhilarating things I've ever done. It's been the single most important project that I've taken on to date. I knew that getting this information out to you with the hope of making a significant change in your life was essential. I wanted to make sure that with every step in The REDLIPSTICK Method, you could easily see how to transition into a greater you. How you could go from feeling invisible to being seen again?

To show up in this process, several things need to happen. As I applied The REDLIPSTICK Method to writing this book, I was able to see my strengths, recognize areas that needed improvement, and observe how I grew. Let me first start off by saying that this was no easy task. I needed to figure out a way to show up despite the fear and doubt. My fear was that I would not be able to articulate this message to you in a way that you could easily follow and yield significant change. I knew that your reading this book could have a profound impact on you and how you move forward from this point. Change is hard, especially the type of change that could have massive results.

When fear and doubt collude, their main goal is to put a stop to whatever it is that you're doing. In essence, their job is to make sure you don't succeed. Oftentimes they throw grenades at your self-esteem. You begin to question or wonder about your abilities. "Who am I to write this book?" As you know, this question came up many times throughout the process for me. Fear and doubt love to offer up a platter of procrastination. There were days I'd mentally prepared to write and the delicious platter of procrastination would overtake me. It was easier to watch the series finale of *Scandal* or to have dinner and a walk on the beach with Khari. But knowing that information in this book was key to eliminating invisibility, I was required to implement all the steps. The Imagine New Life step kept me going because I could see the change in you. Every day I Practiced Affirming it. In the car, in the shower, walking around the beach, I affirmed that you would have this book in your hand. You would have a method to follow to help you feel seen again. Therefore, I had to show up. It wasn't easy, but once I mastered it, I was here. So how did I figure out exactly how to show up? Wait—what does it even mean to show up? I could ask 100 different people and get 100 different explanations, so I am going to share with you what it has meant to me.

How do you show up?

What I found in life and anytime I undertake something is that I need a jolt to get me started. If I don't have the jolt, I tend to put things off. Although I am not a coffee drinker, I tried to condition myself to believe that drinking coffee helps. Not the case, because one cup of coffee, microwaved 3-5 times a day with half the cup still remaining by nightfall, does not equate to a coffee drinker! Therefore, coffee wasn't the thing that gave me the jolt. Then one day I picked up a book called *The 5 Second Rule*. The concepts in this book were key to my solving my procrastination problem. I developed a strategy that worked for me that gave me the jolt I needed to start. First, I set the time and day for my writing. The night before, I reviewed in my head which chapters I was going to be working on and the outcome I expected. Most of my writing was on the weekend, so I'd mentally plan my breaks and meals as well. Once I had visualized the plan, I'd go to bed in a good mood. I was excited about the writing, so when my alarm clock went off, I'd jump up with excitement and follow the visualized schedule.

That's one way I showed up for myself. I assessed what was holding me back (procrastination) from accomplishing my goal, and implemented a plan to address what was found in that self-assessment. Another way I showed up for myself in writing this book was at times when I was confident about writing but I didn't have the motivation to keep going. It was during those times that I'd use various apps on my phone, like the focus wheel, a form of gratitude exercise, to help get the momentum going. I'd start out with what I wanted to achieve and write out truthful positive statements that would ultimately give me the motivation to keep writing.

I found that showing up could be addressed throughout The REDLIPSTICK Method, not just at this point but even near the start of the process. Remember my coaching client, Kathryn? Kathryn was really eager to seek change from feeling broken mentally, physically, emotionally, and spiritually. She wanted this change so badly that she committed to herself that she'd do the work, even when she didn't feel like doing so. Even when she wanted to stay in bed and pull the covers over her head, Kathryn committed to mentally and physically being present. She did this through gratitude exercises. The gratitude exercises improved her mood and thus motivated her to want to change. She was able to conclude that there was more positivity in being seen versus being invisible; thus, her drive to thrive increased. For Mechelle, showing up was easy once she declared her purpose. Taking the leap from being a subordinate to becoming a leader of an unknown workforce was a challenging task. However, she engaged in every step of The REDLIPSTICK Method with the intent of reaching her ultimate goal. Mechelle showed up for herself by identifying her needs and addressing them. She found a mentor, gained skills, and renewed her self-confidence to take the leap. Not only did she apply for a leadership position, she received the offer and accepted the opportunity to lead an international workforce in another country. This was all consistent with the vision board she'd created. Mechelle incorporated gratitude throughout the process and it kept her in a positive mood.

How might you self-sabotage?

When you're not able to show up for yourself, it can present in the form of self-sabotage. Oftentimes it's not done consciously but subconsciously. You may have a fear of success or may not feel confident about how to handle success. For some, because they've had few, if any, major life successes, when victory is near they do something to stop it. Other times, strongholds resurface. If they go unresolved, you can find yourself in a pool of negative emotions and stuck from moving forward.

Showing up for yourself can sometimes mean showing up for yourself at the most vulnerable times. It is at these times when you feel the weakest, when you feel like you can't go forward, when you feel like you're not good enough, or you're not able, capable, competent, or comfortable in doing much of anything. Showing up for yourself during these times takes you back through The REDLIPSTICK Method of Practice Affirming It. Examine what you desire and re-affirm it. Imagine New Life by visualizing what you are striving for and connecting with the emotions of how it will feel once you've manifested it. Going back through these steps gives you the knowledge and the power you need to show up for yourself. Remember you are in control of creating the best version of yourself and in order to do so, you must recognize how you can inadvertently self-sabotage and do the work to show up.

Showing Up and Gratitude

Showing up is big. Showing up is so big that it warrants a response. It required you to take some form of action. When or if you find yourself stuck, move to a mental space where you can show gratitude or thanksgiving. It has the potential to change the outcome in a positive way. It is often said that gratitude is the force multiplier. The more grateful you are, the more you have, and the more you have, the more you are able to do. Also, gratitude creates a space to improve your mood. One way to display gratitude is through prayer and meditation. When you express gratitude, you verbalize what you are grateful or thankful for. With daily or regular practice of gratitude, you reap many benefits. Noted benefits that I and several of my coaching clients have experienced were improved overall mood and increased motivation. It's also contributed to increased self-esteem and improved relationships. Think about it: when you're in a good place and in a good mood, everything concerning you prospers, and people around you get to experience the best version of you, too.

Activity: Show Up—Gratitude Exercise

Purpose: To help influence our emotional state in a positive direction.

Suggested Materials: Paper and pen, or journal and pen, social media

Directions: Create the mood that is conducive to focusing. Spend at least ten minutes journaling about what you are grateful for. Start each sentence with "I am happy …" or "I am grateful …." If using social media to share your gratitude, commit to listing three things for which you are grateful.

Optional Expressive Arts Activity: Gratitude Stone Exercise

Purpose: To help influence our emotional state in a positive direction and connect with the process of art in doing so.

Suggested Materials: Small to medium sized stones, paint pens, and a grateful heart

Directions: Set the mood with relaxing music. Clear any distractions and write and or draw on each stone what you are grateful for.

In a Nutshell

Showing up can be different for you at different steps in the process. Reapply any of the steps as you see necessary. Remember, gratitude is a force multiplier and plays a major role in motivating you to show up when you're struggling. The more grateful you are, the more you are able to do. The more grateful you are, the happier you are. When we desire to grow, showing up is easy. And when you can show up, feeling invisible seems to vanish.

Chapter 11

Transform to the New You

"When your clarity meets your conviction and you apply action to the equation, your world will begin to transform before your eye."
– Lisa Nichols

It's been my experience that people make the best choices with the knowledge they have at the time. People don't wake up choosing to fail or choosing to disappoint. They make life decisions based on their life's experiences. What if life's experiences have been filled with pockets of negativity, sadness, and disappointments? It doesn't constitute the ultimate outcome of a person's life. You get to choose how you want your life to be. Perhaps you didn't realize that in the past, but do you know that your life is a product of your actions? You can transform to the new you based on the knowledge gained through The REDLIPSTICK Method. You are here. You've released the strongholds, you've embraced your authentic selves, you've declared your purpose, you've leaned into the process and set purposeful goals for your lives, you've imagined the new life, you've practiced affirming it, you've shown up, and now you can transform with confidence.

A gentleman asked me, why write a book about being invisible? What message do you want to deliver to people? I told him that in life, many people feel invisible. They erroneously believe that whatever ails them is seen by all and thus they have to work hard to hide it, still going through the motions of the day to day processes. In many cases, our perception of the truth is often skewed. People may have an indication that something is wrong, but it is unlikely that they'd know exactly what's going on unless it's revealed to them. Other times, people work rigorously to appear to be okay. When I was feeling invisible, I made every effort to cover it up as much as possible. I needed to appear normal, like everything was okay. I had a friend who described wanting to feel invisible. She went about the day-to-day operations at home and at work as if everything was okay. She had a lot of job stress and had pressure to perform duties not originally assigned to her when she was first hired. Then, just prior to her reaching out to me, she had received bad news about brother's health. That was the tipping point. She assumed that she needed to be strong for her family and not show her vulnerabilities. She was a supervisor at work and didn't want to appear weak in the office. To her, showing any display of emotional weakness would risk her credibility. So, she just wanted to be invisible.

Reaching out to people, professionals, or resources for help when you need it is not a sign of weakness, it is a sign of strength. I was able to point her in the right direction so that she could have the resources she needed to deal with her brother's health. She was able to bring her family into the situation so that they'd see how to best support one another during this family crisis.

Through incorporating many of the steps found in The REDLIPSTICK Method, she was better able to manage her life's stress and thrive. She realized that reaching out was not a sign of weakness, nor did it have any negative impact on how her family or staff viewed her. She was able to transform to a better version of herself. She no longer desired to be unseen. Embracing her authentic self and using that understanding to determine her self-worth was key in her success. Her faulty thinking and incorrect assumptions created much of the anxiety she chose to take ownership of. When she was able to clearly define her purpose, it was much easier for her to transform into the person she knew she could be.

I could definitely relate to her. When Khari and I found out that we were unable to have children, it was one of the toughest periods in our lives. We had to grow accustomed to the constant questions of when are you going to have a baby, how long is it going to take, tick-tock-tick-tock. When I realized that my purpose was much greater than being a mother, I was able to transform into the person that I was meant to be. I was able to reach people where they were to help them reach their highest potential. This is why I do this work. This is why I know that through my own personal life experiences, transformation is possible. Striving to be visible or invisible in a world that comes with so many challenges can be draining; therefore, choosing to transform and walking in your greatness with confidence is something that you too can achieve.

However, one of the things that was hard for me to say was that I was an author. Actually, I was, in that Khari and I were contributing authors in the book *The Love Pact*, but for some reason, considering myself an independent author was tough. It felt a little vain, so I kept the fact that I was writing this book a secret to most people who knew me and only revealed that I was working on my REDLIPSTICK Project. It wasn't until Khari and I were in a restaurant one day and were having a discussion with some tourists about the East Coast that I admitted it. We'd recently traveled to North Carolina for *The Love Pact* book launch and it came out in the discussion. The lady we were talking to screamed, "I've never met a real live author before," and graciously shook our hands. I was so embarrassed, and Khari was smiling so hard. He was proud to have that title and recognition. Looking back, I believe my discomfort was fear, again, fear of being judged. That seemed to be a theme for me, fear of being judged. Then, as I thought about The REDLIPSTICK Method, I knew that I was in the transformation stage. I needed to transform into the new me. I was a co-author and I was about to become an independent author, so there should be no shame in that. After thinking about that for a while, I quickly felt more confident and embraced this new role. My motivation level advanced even higher.

Mechelle was delighted to embrace her new leadership role and was even more motivated to begin to affect positive change within her team of employees. She often reflected upon walking in her purpose so work became a passion for her. Kathryn also embraced the transformation. She is living more courageously without fear and without the desire to hide.

How to Transform with Confidence

No one knows you better than you know yourself. When you're clear about the change that's about to take place and you've mastered the steps up to this point in The REDLIPSTICK Method, you can move in confidence. You'll feel like nothing can stop you and your self-esteem will soar. Remember, change can be scary, so to fall into this new role can create some resistance, but like I did, as did Kathryn and Mechelle and so many other coaching clients, you've done the work, so embrace this transformation. One thing that I found helpful to me in transforming with confidence was to find a theme song that supported this growth. I chose *This Girl is on Fire* by Alicia Keys. This is the song that I played over and over and it motivated me to embrace this transformation to the new me with confidence.

Activity: Transform to the New You Playlist/Theme Song

Purpose: To connect with music that motivates you in the transformation phase.

Suggested Materials: Music app

Directions: Find that song or songs that resonate with you, that connects you to your life's purpose, that motivates you for this transformation, and listen to it as often as you need to.

Optional Expressive Arts Activity: Transform to the New You—Draw, Paint, Sing, Dance, or Write a Poem

Purpose: To help connect you through expressive art to transform into the new you.

Suggested Materials: Creativity, journal and pen or pen and paper. Paint, brushes, and canvas *or* color writing utensils and paper

Directions: Set the mood. Clear any distractions and create an expression of what transformation looks like to you either through art, song, dance, or poetry.

In a Nutshell

You've got this. You know exactly who you are. All you have to do is embrace this transformation and move into the new you with confidence. Know that you are doing exactly what you have been created to do. This Girl is on Fire.

Chapter 12

Influence Your Surroundings

"Every intention sets energy in motion,
whether you are conscious of it or not."
– Gary Zukav

January 13, 2018 seemed like a normal Saturday. Khari was en route to work and I'd just hung up the phone with my mother. I was preparing to head out for my morning walk but stopped to catch a glimpse of the news. This would be a Saturday I'd never forget.

I live in the state of Hawaii. "Emergency Alert: BALLISTIC MISSILE THREAT INBOUND TO HAWAII. SEEK IMMEDIATE SHELTER. THIS IS NOT A DRILL," displayed across the television. With recent tensions high across the Pacific, this message was believable and seemed surreal all at the same time. With hopes of an error and in great disbelief, I changed the channel to see if it could've possibly been a mistake.

The message was consistent on all stations. I rushed to the telephone to call Khari. He hadn't heard the message so he tuned in to the radio. "Emergency Alert: BALLISTIC MISSILE THREAT INBOUND TO HAWAII. SEEK IMMEDIATE SHELTER. THIS IS NOT A DRILL." He was hearing the same thing. This was in fact real, so I panicked. I had no idea what to do because the message indicated we had fifteen minutes to seek shelter. He instructed me to remain calm. I instantly calmed down, told him I loved him, and found a spot in the house to brace for impact.

The Hawaii Emergency Management Agency inadvertently sent out an alert to thousands of people warning of an inbound ballistic missile. The alert caused widespread panic until the agency was able to issue a corrected message indicating that the alarm was indeed a false alarm.

The thirty-eight minutes it took before a corrected message went out seemed like a lifetime. In reflecting back on that day, I see how Khari's calmness yet stern voice influenced my reaction. His behavior influenced my reaction.

Did you know that your presence, your behavior, and your transformation all have the ability to influence your surroundings? Whether you are in a good place or not, you can influence your surroundings.

When I worked as an academic advisor at the University of North Carolina at Chapel Hill, a student came to see me one day to drop a course. With a baseball cap pulled tightly on her head, barely revealing her eyes, she asked, "Will you please sign this paper so that I can withdraw from this course?" She said she figured she'd have a better chance of passing the course in the summer. She stated the class was very hard and that she was not "Carolina" material. After advising her on her options for summer school, the conversation continued around her lack of social support in the community. She'd indicated she had very few friends and hoped to get connected with a church. We talked about the possibility of going to a popular local church and other ways to connect in the community. The student stated she would look into it. The next time I saw her, it was a year later. She walked into my office and asked if I remembered who she was. I wasn't sure initially because everything about her was different. She reminded me of her situation from the previous year. She confirmed that she was feeling badly about herself at that time—struggling with school—and had considered dropping out.

Amazed at her transformation, I listened to hear more of her story. She went on to say how that encounter with me influenced many things. She reported that later that day, she looked into the church we discussed. She went to the Sunday service and joined the young adult group. She also made friends and joined one of the clubs on campus. She took the class she had dropped that day during the summer session and reported having received an A. The student said that she was motivated and inspired by our encounter and wanted to come back to say "thank you."

We can unintentionally impact those in our path. I didn't hand out any special sauce that day. I was simply being myself, doing my job. Had she never returned to give me an update, I would've never known the level to which she was impacted. There is the power of influence.

The beauty about this is that there are times in which we influence those we have no idea we have actually influenced. When we are able to develop self-love and carry ourselves in a manner in which people are inspired and motivated by it, people are then influenced by us. What this student was describing was consistent with feeling invisible. She wanted to belong but didn't know how. Her life was not going in the right direction and she was about to quit school. This student didn't have a social network but wanted a change. She was receptive to help.

Since we're not always cognizant of how we influence others, we should be mindful to strive to be in a good place all the time. When we operate from a place of authenticity and are moving in our purpose, we are destined to have a positive effect on people. Just the other day, I received a message from a former colleague. The message read: "Hi Rhonda! I want you to know how thankful I am for you. I found the encouraging card you gave me before you left Fort Sill and it reminded me of when you introduced me to the concept of Supernatural childbirth! What happened was nothing short of a miracle and I bless God for knowing you and the impact you have had on my family! I'm grateful for you! Your belief and positivity are infectious and it ignites fires, leaving a legacy for many years to come! Bless you and your family!" Hearing this message served as a confirmation for me that I am doing exactly what I was created to do. I felt validated.

My coaching client Haven, just after she released her strongholds and embraced her authentic self, discovered that she inadvertently influenced her surroundings. She had a friend that was going through a rough divorce as well and when Haven shared about the work she was doing in The REDLIPSTICK Method, her friend became interested in the method and began to work on releasing her erroneous thinking. So influencing your surroundings, just like showing up, can occur at any time in this process.

How do you influence your surroundings?

You too can be an influence in that way. When you influence your surroundings, it is as a result of you doing the work you need for yourself that keeps you in a healthy place. When you have done all the steps in The REDLIPSTICK Method up to this point, you've transformed into the new you. That transformation means you are no longer invisible. Your confidence exudes and people are better able to receive what you might have for them. Although your influence is subconscious, it is genuine and authentic.

What can you choose to declare that has the potential to influence your surroundings? You have authority over what happens in your life moving forward. Therefore, you can choose whatever you want that keeps you in line with your purpose and allows you to influence your surroundings. I choose to have a positive mental attitude. I choose to show up. I choose to move in my purpose. What do you choose?

Activity: Influence Your Surroundings—I Choose Declaration

Purpose: To connect with what you are consciously choosing that keeps you in a good mental space.

Suggested Materials: Journal and pen or pen and paper

Directions: List the things that you are choosing for your life starting with the statement "I choose."

Optional Expressive Arts Activity: Influence Your Surroundings Mandala

Purpose: To have a visual of the commitments you've made to yourself.

Suggested Materials: Markers and paper
Directions: Create an atmosphere conducive to creating. Draw a mandala that connects with influencing your surroundings.

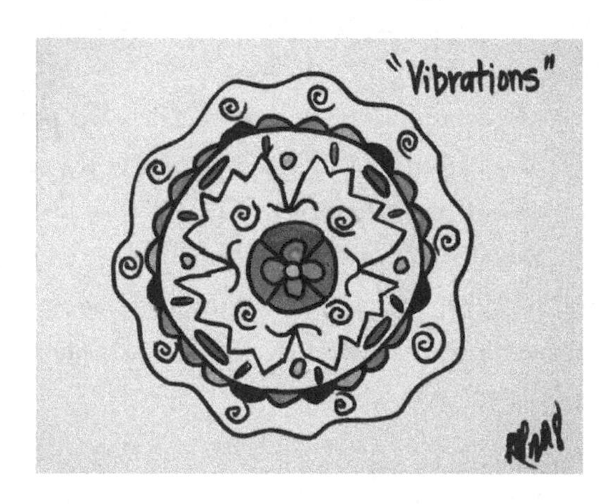

In a Nutshell

No matter what you do, you always influence people around you, whether you are aware of it or not. Believe in your ability to influence others. When you are in a good place, you sow good seeds, and those good seeds take root. The product is good. Remember, make choices that are consistent with positivity so that you can influence positivity in your surroundings. It may make the difference for someone else being seen.

Chapter 13

Celebrate Accomplishments

"The more you praise and celebrate your life, the more there is in life to celebrate."
– Oprah Winfrey

In 2015, I received recognition for Professional of the Year. This particular year, the Professional of the Year was shared with one of my colleagues. It was quite the surprise and such an honor to have received that recognition. We'd exerted a lot of energy and dedicated many hours of hard work executing the duties of our positions. This award came with a monetary gift. I knew I wanted to celebrate and thought that using the money to help fund my goal for professional development would be perfect. Many thoughts came to mind. I wanted to obtain certification for my Laughter Yoga training and weighed my options of looking to go to the UK to receive the instruction, or to go to India to receive the instruction under the Master Laughter Guru himself. After careful consideration, India won. So, I reinvested in myself and booked the trip.

All too often, people focus on what they didn't do to meet their goals or they focus on the shortcomings of their success. They tend to criticize their efforts and pass judgment on their abilities. They may even find that they've developed a lack of confidence in themselves. It's a natural tendency. Acknowledging where you may've fallen short of your success is important. It can better help you understand what you may need to alter to ensure future achievement. You can grow from celebrating your accomplishments. Celebrating your accomplishments not only serves you, but it also serves those within your reach. Your motivation increases, as does the motivation for others around you to succeed. Your self-esteem and confidence are boosted. Celebrating accomplishments also serves as a reminder that you're able to overcome challenges and obstacles that may've been in your way. Celebrating your accomplishments has the potential that when others witness your growth, they tend to want to celebrate with you. These people are your cheerleaders, the ones who want to see you happy and successful. These are the people you want in your life. They are the ones you can influence. However, you may run across those who will have difficulty handling the success in your life. Not everyone is purposed to be a part of your growth. Just know that that's okay because when you accomplish things, you'll gain visibility to those who desire the same things. It has been said too often that we are a combination of the five people we have the closest relationships with. Think about it. There should be two people in your circle that you really grow and develop from and two people who you know you are able to influence. You are that middle person. Everyone benefits and as time continues, you find that your circle changes.

You already know how to influence your surroundings, and celebrating your accomplishments is a way to do so. Having been selected as one of the Professionals of the Year positively impacted one of my friends, Tish. When she learned of the accomplishment, she treated me to an expensive pair of leather boots as a way to say congratulations. She was inspired by the accomplishment, very proud of me, and wanted to celebrate me. Whether you celebrate your own accomplishments or others celebrate you, you tend to experience good emotions. It's because the endorphins that are released give you that incredible positive feeling. Those incredible feelings motivate you to strive for more. The more you celebrate accomplishments, whether big or small, you tend to condition your mind to cultivate positive emotions. Get in the habit of celebrating those small milestones that assist you with reaching your goals.

For those of you who have children or when you are in the presence of someone who has excelled, you tend to delight in celebrating with them. You are proud of their achievements and you may want others to know as well. My parents tell everyone they know when I succeed or accomplish anything. They're always proud of me. Just the other day, I texted my dad "What cha doing?" His response: "Being proud of you." It's statements like that that fuel me to strive to make them even prouder. They celebrate me more than I celebrate myself. How does it make you feel when someone else celebrates you? What about celebrating the accomplishments of others—do you do that? Are you one of those people who is one of the first to celebrate someone else?

You are at the Celebrate Your Accomplishments step in The REDLIPSTICK Method. You have come a long way to get here and all of the things that you've done along the way required your focus, commitment, and desire for something different. Now it's time for you to go celebrate yourself. But first, think back to your last major accomplishment. Reflect on how it felt when you accomplished the goal. If you celebrated, what did you specifically do to celebrate yourself? Was there a time in your life when you accomplished something and didn't celebrate? How did it feel then and, looking back, what are your thoughts about not having celebrated? Do you have any regrets? The reason celebrating yourself is so important is because it allows you to honor your achievements, thus motivating you to do more.

When Kathryn made the big commitment to embrace her authentic self, it warranted a celebration for her. She purchased a piece of nice antique furniture to celebrate her accomplishment. When I completed the steps through the Transform to the New You, I celebrated by treating myself to the spa. Again, it doesn't matter when or how you celebrate, as long as you acknowledge your achievements and celebrate along the way.

Activity: Celebrate Your Accomplishments

Purpose: To acknowledge victory, no matter how big or small, as celebration serves as motivation to continue to strive for what you want.

Suggested Materials: Your choice in whatever method you chose

Directions: Celebrate getting to this point. Or celebrate any recent achievement. Look for big and small achievements. Be mindful of how you choose to celebrate. Choose whatever feels good for you. Feel free to share accomplishments by posting on social media, journal about it, and or tell those people who are important to you all about it.

In a Nutshell

Acknowledging failures provides space for you to grow. Celebrating success reinforces change. It not only reinforces change but it also helps to improve self-esteem. Improved self-esteem motivates you to want to do more. Because you are moving in a direction that supports your life's purpose, all of your accomplishments will have significant meaning. You are longer invisible.

Chapter 14
Kickback

"If you are feeling good, you are thinking good thoughts."
– Rhonda Byrne

You've reached the final step. This is the time where you can truly kickback and play over and over in your mind all that you've done to get to this very point. This is a time where you can bask in the pleasures of hard work and commitment. No matter what it took for you to get to this point, you are more than likely feeling very good about things. It reminds me of the time when I conducted my first international training solo. I had prepared for it well in advance and was more confident than ever about executing it. As with anything you do for the first time, I didn't know what to expect. In looking back, I had already mastered many of the concepts in The REDLIPSTICK Method, so I was really at a good place to deliver. I must admit, it was fabulous. The results were more than I'd expected. Participants were engaged and having fun. They all engaged in rich dialogue for a meaningful training experience. They expressed gratitude and shared how the information provided was thought-provoking for them. Many of the exercises had a creative expressions component to them, so many of the participants explained how engaging in expressive work was relaxing and therapeutic for them. In fact, I had received so much positive feedback that an invitation to return the following year was extended. One of the ways I celebrated the training was to have a nice meal at one of the local fancy restaurants. And what I really remember the most about that experience was after dinner, when I had time alone in my room to take it all in. I reflected upon all that I did to get to that point. The feelings and emotions associated with it were exhilarating. I felt fantastic and so proud of myself. So, you are here now. This step is so significant as it gives you space to reflect and honor your hard work. Everything you've done to show up and to make this transformation real is what's important here. You're responsible for this success, so kickback. You have the results that you were looking for. You no longer have to feel invisible.

Mechelle treated herself to a trip to Indonesia. It was there that she spent time under a palm tree basking in the knowledge that she's living the life she desired. Once she released her stronghold of guilt, so many things moved so fast for her. Mechelle was grateful for her transformation and now has a specific method to follow and steps to apply at any time in her life.

For me, writing this chapter in this book was a humbling experience. I have such a strong desire to head down to the lagoon and bask in the knowledge that I showed up. I went through this process just like you did or will do, and to reflect back on it, is a magical treat. I still can't believe I moved from not believing I could write this book to now, just a few chapters away from completion.

Remember the song by Irene Cara, "What a Feeling?" I can't seem to get the words out of my head: "What a Feeling … Bein's believin' … I can have it all … Now I'm dancing for my life." This is exactly where you're at. You've mastered the steps in The REDLIPSTICK Method to help you erase the feeling of invisibility. You have all of the steps necessary to ensure that you will be seen.

Imagine yourself sitting on the beach, watching the waves, and listening to the sound of the oceans crashing against the rocks. You are breathing in the fresh air as you soak up the sunrays at just the right temperature. You're taking it all in as you begin to reflect back upon what it's taken to get you to this very point. The Kickback step can be personal and quite emotional. You may have gone through a transformation that you'll never forget. Trust the process, enjoy this journey. You are exactly where you're supposed to be. I love Rhonda Byrne's quotes about how, if you are feeling good, then you are thinking good thoughts. The more positive you can be, the more you attract positive things into your life. This blissful moment, like when you celebrated your accomplishments, builds confidence. It's proof that you can do exactly what you've set out to do. Bask in the magnificence of now being seen.

Activity: Kickback

Purpose: To spend time reflecting back on your accomplishments and connecting with the feelings associated with the achievements.

Suggested Materials: Journal and pen or pen and paper

Directions: Write about your experience. Reflect on the process and write it out. Remember to note how you feel.

Optional Activity: Kickback

Purpose: To spend time reflecting back on the accomplishments and connecting with the feelings associated with your achievements.

Suggested Materials: Comfortable space

Directions: Create an atmosphere conducive for relaxing. Sit or lie down in a comfortable position. Put on your favorite relaxing music. Spend some time reflecting on your journey and take note of how you are feeling. Be cognizant of your breathing.

In a Nutshell

Kicking back not only allows you to reflect on your progress but it also reminds that you can do that which you set out to do. It gives you space to experience those moments of achievement, thus motivating you to continue to strive for what you want in life. Relax, let go, and allow the manifestation of being seen take root.

Chapter 15
The Hurdle

"Often, people who can do, don't, because they're afraid of what people who can't do, will say about them doing it."
– Trevor Noah

Red Lipstick now has a new meaning. Who would've ever thought that applying Red Lipstick could be so transformational? Ladies, at times we all find something about ourselves or our circumstances that we want to change or improve but because we feel or have felt invisible, we don't change it. Perhaps it's because we feel stuck or don't know where to start. Or maybe we're afraid of what others may say. For some of us, feeling invisible may have been more comfortable or choosing to be invisible may have felt safe, but this does not have to be you. Change can happen. You may have read a self-help book and thought, "This is an excellent idea" and even planned to follow some of the steps. The intentions are good and you get energized for the first few days or weeks. You may even implement what you've learned, but then something occurs. Or maybe you start the process and realize that you're actually changing and that's scary. Self-sabotage is real. "Life" happens, so somehow your follow-through prevents your breakthrough. But you can do this. In fact, while writing this book I often wondered if I should stop or start over from a different angle or start over with a different message. This book had been on my mind every day and every night, when I laid down at night and when I woke up in the morning. All I saw was you. I saw you being visible to not only the world but to yourself. I saw you transforming in every chapter. You were my motivation. My choice to invest in a coach during this process was solely because I wanted the best from me, to give to you. You were my reason, so you can do this. You have the tools to be successful. You have a specific method to follow that will get you the results you are looking for. I won't be surprised if you'll discover things about yourself that you never realized. I'm talking about your inner strength. Discovering that you're more powerful than you thought and that you can walk in confidence no matter where you are or who you're with.

I've provided for you a specific outline to take you through the process. You can engage at your own pace but remember to have a plan to overcome obstacles for when life gets in the way. Many people have greater success following a program when they have someone who can help hold them accountable and keep them on track. If that's you, you can connect with someone and go through The REDLIPSTICK Method together. It is my recommendation that you don't go at it alone. Identify that accountability partner or reach out to a coach. When I'm coaching clients we tend to get better results at a faster rate than when they work on their own. The cathartic process, especially in step one, allows clients to create space that really nurtures transformation. Releasing the strongholds by identifying and letting go of the faulty thinking has been powerful. It truly is the foundation for change and growth.

Chapter 16

Recap and the Call to Join The REDLIPSTICK Movement

"When you know better you do better."
– Maya Angelou

I saw a post from one of my friends on social media that read: "Women who invest in themselves go further." In fact, not only do women go further but they go further *faster* when they invest in themselves. For many of us, it may be difficult because we're conditioned to believe that family is always first. Who am I to consider myself more important or valuable than my family, my children, right? It's not that you're more important, but rather, you're just as important, because in order to give the best of yourself, you must take good care of yourself, which includes assessing areas in your life that need work and getting connected to the resources to do it. If you have a need to work on something or engage in self-care, it's impossible to give 100% or the best version of yourself when there's lack. I'm here to tell you that from many years of experience, it's better to serve people when you are full. Full of confidence, full of energy, full of passion, full of love, full of self-love, full of desire, and if that means investing in taking care yourself, taking care of your needs, I commission you.

As you can see, this hasn't been about getting the accolades from work or getting the attention from your companion, it's solely about who it is that you desire to be, examining ways to grow from the inside out, then achieving it. This has been about you changing organically. Transforming on a cellular level. So whether it's feeling invisible, feeling broken, feeling insecure, feeling devalued, feeling guilty, feeling lonely, feeling depressed, feeling anxious, or whatever you are experiencing that you want to change, it can happen.

Think for a minute. What is your REDLIPSTICK moment? Remember, my REDLIPSTICK moment was when I realized I was rejecting things I'd never even tried. I blocked the opportunities and never gave myself a chance to explore. Can you find your REDLIPSTICK moment? Have there been times where you have felt invisible or have closed the door to opportunities that you thought were not meant for you?

Remember, I felt invisible as well, but now I no longer have to and neither do you.

Join me in this REDLIPSTICK Movement. The magic of doing this program is the ability to connect with your inner self and move into a place where you are confident and able to achieve things that are aligned with your life's purpose. Step out into your greatness.

The bonus of doing the optional expressive arts exercises allows you to walk away with something tangible, something you created from a place authentically. I have outlined an easy process for you to follow. Again, you can do it alone or you can work with me. Choosing to work with me allows you the opportunity to dig deeper in making a significant change that will not only allow you to stop being invisible but will also give you the confidence required to be amazing no matter where you are.

So, take radical action now. All you have to do is to apply The REDLIPSTICK Method and watch how you begin to transform into feeling seen again in every aspect of your life. If you have a tube of red lipstick, go to the mirror and apply it. Watch how you transform. If you don't have a tube of red lipstick, I encourage you to join up with your mother, grandmother, auntie, daughter, sister, niece, cousin, best friend, girlfriend, coworker, mentor or whoever it may be, but go find that red lipstick. Remember, you don't need the red lipstick to show the world who you are, but rather the red lipstick is symbolic for you so that when you look in the mirror, you are reminded that change is possible and you are no longer invisible.

Once that magical tube of red lipstick is in your possession, apply it immediately, because releasing the strongholds; embracing your authentic self; declaring your purpose; leaning into the process; imagining new life; practicing affirming it; showing up; transforming into the new you; influencing your surroundings; celebrating your accomplishments; and kicking back will all begin to become second nature to you.

If you are on social media, no matter which social media platform, put on your magical red lipstick and post a picture proudly, adding the hashtags #VISIBLE, #REDLIPSTICK. Today is a new day and we can all be seen again. Let's start by eliminating the feelings of invisibility so that we can all master the art of being seen. #VISIBLE, #REDLIPSTICK

Acknowledgments

Where do I start? Writing this book has been quite the spiritual journey. From the depths of my soul I thank God for choosing me for this assignment. I'm most appreciative for the angels God strategically appointed to me in this process for they have been by my side every step of the way. For this, I'm humbly grateful.

I know my steps are ordered and when it was clear that Dr. Angela Lauria was going to lead me in the process of getting this book out, I knew I found favor with the Lord. Watching in silence, I learned more than you know, Angela. Thanks for changing the world, thousands of people at a time. For you certainly master the step of influencing your surroundings. And for your awesome team of professionals who were key in the success of this project, I thank each of you.

To the Morgan James Publishing team: Special thanks to David Hancock, CEO & Founder for believing in me and my message. To my Author Relations Manager, Margo Toulouse, thanks for making the process seamless and easy. Many more thanks to everyone else, but especially Jim Howard, Bethany Marshall, and Nickcole Watkins.

Life wouldn't exist in its fullness if it weren't for my husband, Khari Kaalund, who supports and protects me in every aspect. I am a better person because of you and this book wouldn't have been written if it weren't for your belief in me and unconditional love and support.

I must've been about five or six years old when my mother, Sandra Peterson, told me that I could do anything I put my mind to or could be anything I wanted to be. When she speaks, I believe her, because somehow it always seems that what she speaks over me, comes true. From an early age, I observed her pray and noticed that her prayers would get answered. Because of this, I solicited her prayers when I needed a divine intervention. This book required a divine intervention, so I asked my mother; my mother-in-law—Jackie Mburu—and my husband to intercede on my behalf. To you three, words cannot express my gratitude for your diligence in praying for the perfection of this project every single day at 10 p.m. Eastern Standard Time. Jackie, thank you for praying even when you were not feeling so well. Your commitment made all the difference. Nothing is impossible when the Lord is included, so I thank you for that vital role.

Thank you to my dad, James Little, for always praying for me, believing in me, making me feel special, and showing me that I am loved.

My motivation to write this book was for my sister Tabatha Jones, who is my rock, who has always been my friend from beginning of time. And my best friend forever, Kathleen Wiener, who supports me unconditionally. I can never imagine life without the two of you, for your love for me drives me to do the work that I do. Thank you both for believing in me.

It is a blessing to have such treasured relationships with my two favorite girls in the world, my nieces Cassie Peterson and Kholi Jones. Thanks for holding space for me to have an important part in your lives. I hope this book can take you both further, faster.

For the unwavering support obtained from my mentee, Dequilah Brandon, all the way from China. Thanks for jumping in and assisting me on all of the projects I have going on. I love your passion to help others and I'm so aware of how you influence your surroundings. I hope you are able to see it too. Thanks for being your authentic self. I'm confident that your best is yet to come.

To my silent supporters Hayva Hill, RaShonda Labrador, and Nashay Lorick. Thank for your contributions to this project. I value you so much.

To my friend, Petra Richardson. Chatting with you daily about the book process was so very motivational for me. Your excitement and enthusiasm fueled my energy so I thank you for your support.

To my little brother, Vincent Calvert Mondell Little. Thanks for checking in on me daily, asking, "What are you doing?" and me responding, "Writing." It's finally over, at least for now, so my responses when you check in with me will be, "Helping people transform, one person at a time."

To Sherie Aaron, who held me accountable for two years on writing the book that was inside of me. You played such an instrumental role in keeping me focused on the end results and I will always be grateful to you for that.

My sincerest gratitude goes to Cinda Robison. I would've never pursued this assignment in this way had it not been for our amazing life talks. You have no idea how instrumental you have been in this process. Therefore, to you I am forever grateful. Thank you for everything.

And finally, to you, my ideal reader. I have waited for this moment for us to meet at this point. I see your transformation happening already. The world is waiting for you to be seen.

I love each and every one of you for how you have touched me.

About the Author

Rhonda Kaalund has an exceptional gift for unveiling the invisible. She uses a unique method to help walk clients through a process where they dive deep within themselves to root out negative thought patterns and paradigms and rewire that which had been hardwired.

With over 20 years of experience assisting people in defeating their limitations, Rhonda has embedded her footprint on both a national and international stage. She has facilitated dynamic trainings, workshops, and mentoring opportunities to hundreds of people across the globe.

Rhonda has a passion for enhancing emotional wellness. She is a Certified Laugher Yoga teacher. Rhonda uses aspects of Laughter Yoga in her work to help others cultivate happier meanings in life.

Rhonda has a Master of Arts Degree in Community Counseling with a concentration in the Expressive Arts Therapies from Appalachian State University. She is a Licensed Professional Counselor, a Licensed Clinical Addictions Specialist, and a Certified Employee Assistance Professional. Rhonda is a member of Delta Sigma Theta Sorority, Inc.

Rhonda and her husband Khari are co-authors in *The Love Pact*, a book of stories on marriage resilience exploring how they have sustained marital bliss. Assisting people and couples in becoming the best versions of themselves is a true passion for Rhonda.

Rhonda lives in Hawaii on the beautiful island of Oahu with Khari. When she is not busy helping others transform organically, she enjoys indulging in the expressive arts, spending time in the library, taking pictures of beautiful scenery, and traveling around the world.

Facebook—https://www.facebook.com/rhonda.kaalund

Instagram—https://www.instagram.com/rhondakaalund

Linked In—https://www.linkedin.com/in/rhonda-kaalund-b20608141

Twitter—https://twitter.com/KaalundRhonda

Email—visible@rhondakaalund.com

Website—https://www.rhondapkaalund.com/

Thank You

Thank you for choosing to spend time reading this book. I know that change requires a conscious effort and I also know that change is easier to make when you are not going at it alone. The gateway to being seen is through the realization that you were never in fact invisible, you simply needed your eyes to open.

If you're ready to stop feeling invisible, then The REDLIPSTICK Method is right for you. Let's discuss further on a free strategy call. Simply send an email to visible@rhondakaalund.com with "Strategy Call" in the subject line and I'll reach out soon.

If you are unsure The REDLIPSTICK Method is right for you, check out this quiz at: https://goo.gl/forms/4XFn8BAH99wvbPYU2 to see where you stand.

Also follow me on the various social media sites to see the latest happenings with this Red Lipstick Movement.

Facebook—https://www.facebook.com/rhonda.kaalund
Instagram—https://www.instagram.com/rhondakaalund
Linked In—https://www.linkedin.com/in/rhonda-kaalund-b20608141
Twitter—https://twitter.com/KaalundRhonda
Email—visible@rhondakaalund.com
Website—https://www.rhondapkaalund.com/

Printed in the USA
CPSIA information can be obtained
at www.ICGtesting.com
JSHW012013140824
68134JS00024B/2390

9 781642 793390